TORNADOES

Shirley Duke

Rourke
Educational Media

rourkeeducationalmedia.com

Scan for Related Titles
and Teacher Resources

Before Reading:

Building Academic Vocabulary and Background Knowledge

Before reading a book, it is important to tap into what your child or students already know about the topic. This will help them develop their vocabulary, increase their reading comprehension, and make connections across the curriculum.

1. Look at the cover of the book. What will this book be about?
2. What do you already know about the topic?
3. Let's study the Table of Contents. What will you learn about in the book's chapters?
4. What would you like to learn about this topic? Do you think you might learn about it from this book? Why or why not?
5. Use a reading journal to write about your knowledge of this topic. Record what you already know about the topic and what you hope to learn about the topic.
6. Read the book.
7. In your reading journal, record what you learned about the topic and your response to the book.
8. After reading the book complete the activities below.

Content Area Vocabulary
Read the list. What do these words mean?

Doppler radar
forecast
Fujita Scale
funnel cloud
interdisciplinary
mesocyclone
meteorologists
simulator
supercells
updraft
wall clouds

After Reading:

Comprehension and Extension Activity

After reading the book, work on the following questions with your child or students in order to check their level of reading comprehension and content mastery.

1. Explain the differences and similarities of a gustnado, dust devil, and tornado. (Summarize)
2. What information is used to determine a tornado rating? (Asking questions)
3. Why should you listen to weather services during severe weather? (Text to self connection)
4. How do meteorologists and storm chasers work together? (Summarize)
5. Describe the different shapes a tornado makes. Is one more destructive than another? Explain. (Visualize)

Extension Activity

Is where you live prone to tornadoes? Do you have other natural disasters in your area? Having an emergency plan and emergency kit is essential. Create an emergency plan for your home and an emergency kit. What would you include in your kit and why? Where's the safest place in your home during a natural disaster like a tornado? Why is it the safest place?

Table of Contents

Tornado!

A thunderstorm blasts rainwater against the window. Hail falls from the sky and lands with a bounce. A dark twisting shape drops from the gray-black cloud. Time to take cover—it's a tornado!

A tornado is a column of air that rotates powerfully and drops from a thundercloud to the ground. Not every storm produces tornadoes. Storms vary in the amounts of rain, hail, lightning, and winds they produce. Some spin out tornadoes.

Large tornadoes can have winds as fast as 300 miles (483 kilometers) per hour. They blow trees from the ground, lift cars, and damage buildings and roofs.

Tornadoes occur on the ground and cause damage there. A **funnel cloud** rotates in the same cone shape. It comes from clouds but it does not touch ground or cause any damage. Still, it can become a tornado if it drops down far enough.

All tornadoes look somewhat different. They can be funnel-shaped, ropy, or wide like a wedge. Wind is clear, but most tornadoes have color. The color depends on the soil and debris they move over and pick up.

Tornadoes may be difficult to spot in heavy rain. An F3 tornado with winds up to 200 miles per hour (321.9 kilometers per hour) in 2006 near Wynne, Arkansas, destroyed several houses, mobile homes, and grain silos.

Tornadoes may look gray with rain, black, or white. The red dirt of Oklahoma sometimes makes the tornadoes look red. Some are so clear they are hard to see. They can even have more than one funnel.

Tornadoes are unpredictable. They can move from any direction. Most move from southwest to northeast. A few move west to east. Their paths can change directions or even turn around.

Short-lived tornadoes may last a few seconds but some can last up to an hour. Most tornadoes last between five and ten minutes before they break up.

A tornado may sound like a rumbling train. It also could make a roaring or whooshing sound. Large tornadoes can sound like a jet overhead.

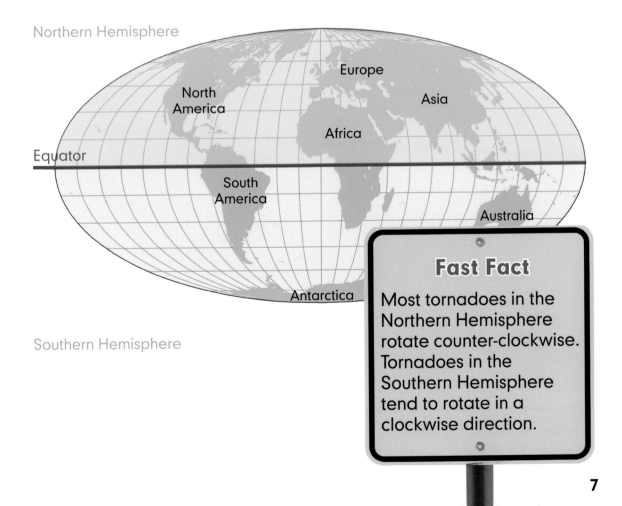

Northern Hemisphere

Europe

North America

Asia

Africa

Equator

South America

Australia

Antarctica

Southern Hemisphere

Fast Fact

Most tornadoes in the Northern Hemisphere rotate counter-clockwise. Tornadoes in the Southern Hemisphere tend to rotate in a clockwise direction.

The United States has about 1,200 tornadoes each year. Records weren't kept until 1950 so accurate estimates aren't fully known. Canada has about 100 per year.

Tornadoes have occurred in every US state. Some states have more than others. They tend to develop in areas between the latitudes of 30 degrees and 50 degrees. These regions have cold air meeting with warm air. The normal wind speeds are often different. This helps set up rotation patterns in storms.

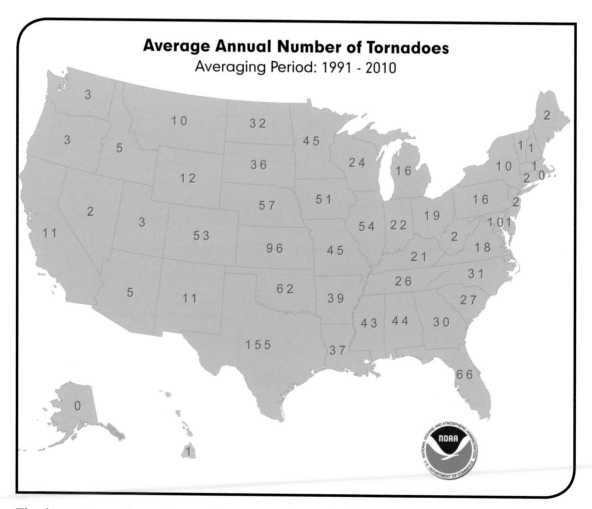

The largest number of tornadoes occur through the central US, between the Rocky Mountains and the Appalachian Mountains.

States in the central US have a higher than average number of tornadoes. This area is nicknamed Tornado Alley.

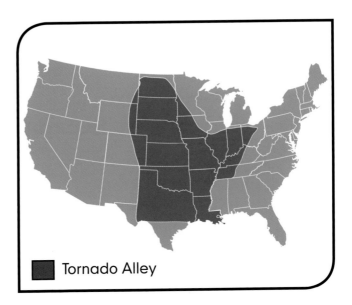

Tornado Alley

Most tornadoes develop during tornado season, although they can form at any time of the year. May through June is a peak time for the Southern Plains region. The Northern Plains and the Midwest have more tornadoes in June and July. Tornadoes most often take place between 4 p.m. and 9 p.m. but can occur at any time.

The best way to avoid a waterspout is to move at a 90 degree angle to its apparent movement. Never move close to investigate a waterspout. Some can be just as dangerous as tornadoes.

Fast Fact

A waterspout is a tornado over water. They are common over southern Florida and the Keys. Marine warnings are issued when waterspouts are seen over waters by the coast. They don't count officially as a tornado unless they reach land. Waterspouts can be dangerous. They turn boats over, cause damage to ships, and injure people.

How Tornadoes Form

Every day, **meteorologists** predict the weather. Tornadoes develop from certain weather conditions. The conditions often include a storm.

A mass of warm, moist air from the Gulf of Mexico meets cool, dry Canadian and Rocky Mountain air. The atmosphere becomes unstable. The lighter, warm air moves upward and the heavier, cold air mass moves in under the warm. This creates thunderstorms.

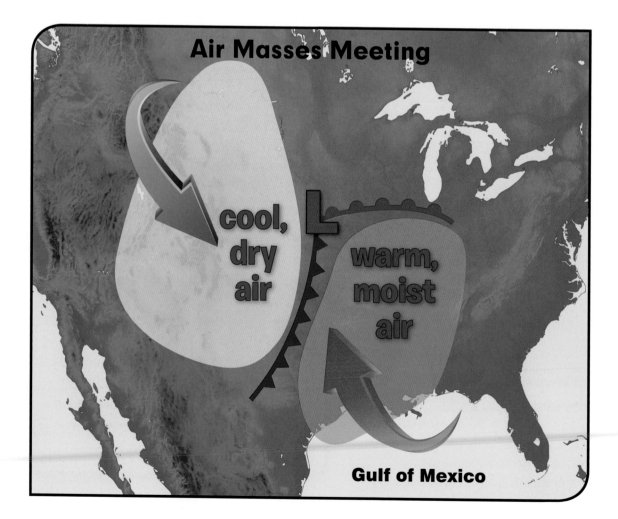

Air Masses Meeting

cool, dry air

warm, moist air

Gulf of Mexico

Supercell storms are the rarest and most dangerous storms. They contain rotating updrafts and are more organized than regular storms.

Not every thunderstorm forms a tornado. The strongest tornadoes develop from **supercells**. These are thunderstorms with rotating circulation inside. The air is moving upward in the rotation. The supercells can be seen on radar.

This circulating air column is called a **mesocyclone**. Supercells bring heavy hail, strong winds, lightning, and flash floods.

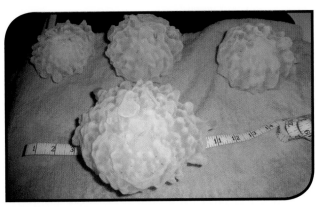

A thunderstorm in Vivian, South Dakota, produced a record-sized hailstone. It measured eight inches (20.3 centimeters) in diameter and weighed one pound, 15 ounces (.9 kilograms). The circumference was 18⅓ inches (47 centimeters).

Mesocyclone Formation

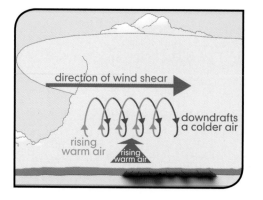

1. Less dense, rising warm air meeting dense, sinking cold air causes wind shear, shown in red, when they meet. The change in air direction mixes the two masses and air starts to spin horizontally.

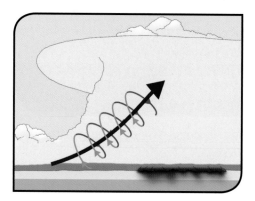

2. The rising warm air, shown in blue, pulls the spinning air upward to create a vertical column inside the cloud.

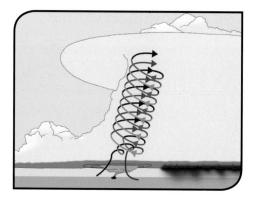

3. The spinning column of air can pick up speed during the rotation, making the spirals tighten, much like the way ice skaters spin faster by pulling in their arms. This forms the mesocyclone.

Meteorologists don't know exactly how this causes tornadoes. A hook echo that develops on radar images can show a tornado forming. The hook echo isn't always a clear shape, but it shows rotation. A hook echo means a mesocyclone is moving in the supercell.

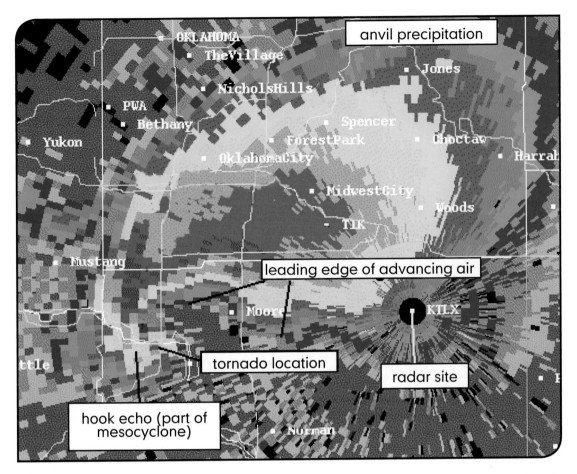

anvil precipitation

leading edge of advancing air

tornado location

radar site

hook echo (part of mesocyclone)

This Oklahoma City NEXRAD radar image from May 3, 1999, shows a supercell storm with a strong tornado in it. The classic hook echo is clearly seen on the left of the radar image.

Wall clouds bulge below a thunderstorm base. They come from a strong **updraft** of rain-cooled air in a thunderstorm. The mass rotates before tornadoes or funnel clouds drop down from them.

Wall clouds are on the southwest side of the storm. They are about one to four miles (1.6 to 6.4 kilometers) across.

NOAA National Weather Service meteorologists study and predict the weather and its effects on climates. Their jobs vary, and they also participate in atmosphere research, teaching, and broadcasting.

Be a Tornado Forecaster

Anyone who wants to be a tornado forecaster should love stormy weather and be interested in tornadoes. Storm forecasters need to be well-educated in atmosphere science and meteorology. Forecasters read science journals to learn new developments in the field. Years of experience help them know what data is important.

How tornadoes break apart isn't clear, either. Tornadoes need unstable air, heat, or moisture, along with a rotation, to continue. A change in any of these factors can break it up. Some thunderstorms grow weak after the cold air flows out of its rainy area.

Meteorologists from the Severe Thunderstorm Electrification and Precipitation Study (STEPS) ready a weather balloon for launch into a large Kansas thunderstorm containing a tornado. The balloon holds tools to measure temperature, wind speed, air pressure, and electrical charges inside the thunderstorm.

Tornadoes are difficult to **forecast**. A forecast is a prediction of what the weather will be. Meteorologists combine computer models with observations and a knowledge of patterns to make a forecast.

Observations come from the ground and upper air through weather instruments and air balloon reports. Satellites provide pictures of clouds. This data is fed into computers and plotted on weather maps. Then meteorologists figure out the weather forecast.

Severe weather can't be predicted very far ahead of time. Predictions have improved enough to warn people a short time ahead of a tornado. This has saved many lives.

The National Weather Service (NWS) supplies tornado forecasts in the US. Tornado warnings are supplied by the Storm Prediction Center in Norman, Oklahoma. They work with the National Oceanic and Atmospheric Administration (NOAA) there.

Weather and storm forecasting began in the early 1950s. Radar allowed meteorologists to see rain and snow. Radar uses radio energy to send out a signal. The reflections sent back show the direction and distance of things.

How Weather Radar Works

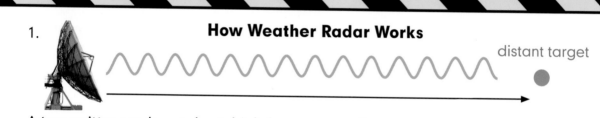

1. A transmitter sends out short, high frequency radio waves or microwaves in the direction of a target object. Then the radar turns off the transmitter and the receiver turns on. This on and off transmission is set at a certain speed.

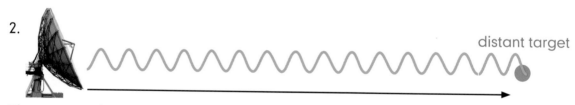

2. The waves, which can travel a long distance and move at the speed of light, hit the target. Waves that directly hit the object reflect, returning to the receiver, much like the way a sound echo returns a voice.

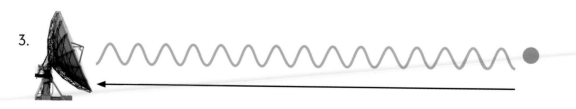

3. The radar measures the time it takes for the echo to return and its strength, along with other information, and then analyzes the image.

Doppler radar use began in the 1960s. It shows precipitation in thunderstorms and how fast they are moving. It shows how heavy the precipitation is, hail size, and rainfall amounts. It does this by measuring the changes in the signal frequency it receives back.

The NWS is using a new Doppler radar called Next Generation Radar (NEXRAD). It lets meteorologists see different storm views and predict storm severity.

Scientists study tornadoes and keep records about them. Learning about tornadoes and tracking them helps forecast them.

The NWS NEXRAD Radar Center is in Norman, Oklahoma, at the National Storm Prediction Center. NEXRAD radar sites are located across the country to track weather and help forecast it.

Measuring Tornadoes

Weather data records help predict storms and tornadoes. Tornado scientists use different kinds of knowledge to study and record tornadoes.

Tornadoes develop into different sizes and shapes. Weak tornadoes last from one to ten minutes. Their winds stay under 110 miles (177.03 kilometers) per hour. About two-thirds of all tornadoes are weak. Winds this speed can still cause damage.

Tornado Records	
most in one calendar day	April 27, 2011; 209 tornadoes
most in one month	April 2011; 817 tornadoes
deadliest tornado	May 22, 2011; EF-5 tornado, Joplin, Missouri, 158 direct fatalities
deadliest year	2011; 519 killed
city hit by most tornadoes	Oklahoma City, 100 tornadoes earliest recorded in 1893
greatest outbreak	greatest swarm of tornadoes 175, April 27-28, 2011
state with most tornadoes	Texas, averages 125 tornadoes
month with most tornadoes	May, followed by June
biggest known tornado	El Reno, Oklahoma, May 31, 2013, 2.6 mile (4.2 kilometer) wide path

Strong tornadoes last about 20 minutes. Their winds reach between 110 and 205 miles per hour (177–330 kilometers per hour). Just under a third of tornadoes that form are strong tornadoes.

Only a small fraction of the remaining tornadoes are violent. They may last an hour or more. Their winds blow more than 205 miles (330 kilometers) per hour and are extremely damaging.

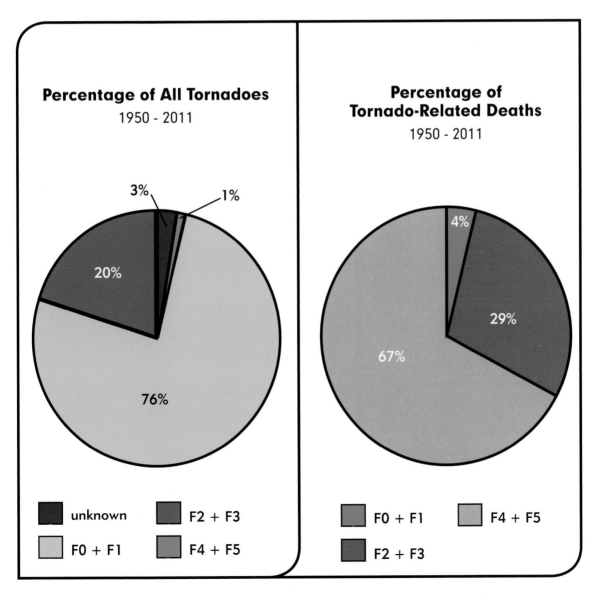

Percentage of All Tornadoes
1950 - 2011

3%   1%
20%
76%

unknown   F2 + F3
F0 + F1   F4 + F5

Percentage of Tornado-Related Deaths
1950 - 2011

4%
29%
67%

F0 + F1   F4 + F5
F2 + F3

Fast Fact

A gustnado is a short, weak whirlwind at the front of a set of gusty winds. They can pick up dust but are not tornadoes.

A dust devil forms in the heat. They are whirlwinds begun by light, dry breezes. They make a swirl of dust moving about 70 miles (113 kilometers) per hour. They aren't tornadoes because they don't form from a thunderstorm or any cloud.

The highest wind speed measured was 295 miles (475 kilometers) per hour in the El Reno, Oklahoma tornado in 1999. But it is hard to measure tornado wind speeds because of the damage they bring. They usually destroy recording instruments, so it's not absolutely known what speeds are reached in any tornado.

Ted Fujita at the University of Chicago developed a rating method for tornadoes in 1971. He worked with Allen Pearson. The early **Fujita Scale** assigned a category using F and the numbers one through five. A mild tornado was an F1. A strong tornado was an F4 or F5. A team of meteorologists and wind engineers updated the Fujita Scale in 1973 to include the path size.

Tetsuya Theodore "Ted" Fujita was born in 1920 in Japan. He graduated with a degree in mechanical engineering. After bombs were dropped on Hiroshima and Nagasaki in 1945, he investigated the ruins. This work was the beginning of his future science investigations.

He decided to become a meteorologist and started teaching in the US in 1946. He researched meteorology and focused on storms. He developed the Fujita Scale with its estimates of wind speed from wind damage. He upgraded it years later, after further study.

Fujita also discovered downbursts and microbursts, which are falling columns of cold air that mimic tornado damage and can cause plane crashes. He taught at the University of Chicago until his death in 1998.

In 2007 the Enhanced Fujita Scale came into use. It includes more variables, with 28 damage indicators such as building type, trees, and structural damage.

Each damage indicator has eight types of damage. They range from visible damage to completely destroyed. The decisions for ratings are based on the observations of scientists.

Tornadoes rated on the early scale have kept their rating for historical value. Some values were adjusted to fit with the new Enhanced Fujita Scale. The earlier ratings for wind speeds might be somewhat lower than they were stated.

A home was lifted off its foundation, rotated, and dropped by an EF-2 tornado in an Oregon Township on March 15, 2012. The family inside sheltered under a couch and no one was hurt.

F-Scale			EF-Scale	
Rating	Wind Speed	Damage	Rating	Wind Speed
F0	<73 mph	Light Damage	EF-0	65-85 mph
F1	73-112 mph	Moderate Damage	EF-1	86-110 mph
F2	113-157 mph	Significant Damage	EF-2	111-135 mph
F3	158-206 mph	Severe Damge	EF-3	136-165 mph
F4	207-260 mph	Devastating Damage	EF-4	166-200 mph
F5	261-318 mph	Incredible Damage	EF-5	+200 mph

The original Fujita Scale was revised to include different standards for measuring tornadoes.

An EF-5 tornado hit Joplin, Missouri, on June 15, 2011. This school was completely destroyed. The mile-wide tornado with winds over 200 miles per hour (322 kilometers per hour) crushed and lifted homes, schools, and commercial and industrial buildings.

Whatever shape a tornado takes, it is formed in a similar way. Different weather conditions cause the changes in appearance. More than one tornado may develop from the same supercell.

Tornadoes develop as a spinning column in a funnel shape. They can widen into a wedge that can be as wide as it is tall. Others twist thin and have a rope-like shape.

The rating of a tornado's violence doesn't depend on its size or shape. Large, wide tornadoes can do little damage while a small, ropy tornado can be an EF-4 or EF-5 and do tremendous damage.

The NWS offices issues tornado information. Local news stations broadcast warnings to affected areas.

A tornado watch means tornadoes are possible. A tornado warning means a tornado has been spotted on the ground or with Doppler radar. People in warning areas should take cover right away.

Lead forecaster Rich Thompson with the NWS Storm Prediction Center identifies a potential tornado and sends out a tornado watch for Kansas and Nebraska. This center monitors weather for the United States and issues watches and warnings when needed.

Before and After

Prepare for a tornado before it happens. It's especially important if you live in areas with frequent tornadoes. Have a family disaster plan. Discuss where to go during a tornado.

Many homes have basements. This is the best place to wait out a tornado. If you don't have a basement, go to an inside room or closet without windows on the lowest floor. Get under a piece of strong furniture.

Flying debris can be more dangerous than wind. Leave windows closed. Open windows allow wind and debris to fly inside.

Flying debris from tornadoes act like missiles and can penetrate bodies and buildings easily. Flying debris causes many injuries during a tornado. Taking cover or getting into a sheltered place is the best way to protect yourself.

Some people put safe rooms in their homes. These small, reinforced concrete and steel rooms give extra protection during tornadoes. They fit in basements or on the ground floor.

Some cities have community shelters designed to protect a large number of people.

Tornado safe rooms are specially hardened rooms or structures with reinforced walls. These shelters are designed to FEMA standards and offer the best possible protection during a tornado.

Keep a battery radio nearby for new information. Watch the weather during storms and be prepared to take cover if needed.

People living in mobile homes should find shelter. The mobile homes don't give any protection during a tornado.

Experts agree the best protection during a tornado is underground. This new design for a storm shelter protected the residents of this home during a May 20, 2013, EF-5 tornado.

If a tornado hits, stay in your shelter until the storm has passed. Check your home for damage. The power may be out, so use a flashlight from your emergency kit.

Treat any injuries in your family and get help if the injuries are serious or people are trapped under debris. Don't move a seriously injured person.

If riding in the car, stop and get out of it. Go to a ditch or the lowest area around and lie down. Wait until the storm passes.

Some people think stopping a car under a bridge makes for good shelter. It does not. Debris can fly around and gets trapped there. People can be blown from under the bridge and out into the storm.

Any kind of vehicle can be deadly during a tornado. They give a larger surface to the wind and can be picked up and carried for a short distance or thrown into a tree.

Outside, stay away from downed power lines and gas lines. Many injuries are caused by people entering damaged buildings and climbing on debris during clean-up. Wear protective clothing and heavy shoes or boots. Watch for broken glass and nails. Stay away from areas with damage.

If your home is damaged, shut off all power and gas lines. Let the power company know what has happened.

The Red Cross and Salvation Army have resources to help. Local volunteer groups may offer assistance, too. Churches and nonprofit organizations often pitch in to help. The Federal Emergency Management Agency (FEMA) responds to and supports emergency aid.

American Red Cross volunteers like Adriana Persenaire, pictured here, help provide immediate aid and comfort following a disastrous storm to survivors like Sandra Simmons, who lost her home in a tornado.

Know the Tornado Signs
- dark sky with a green color
- rotation in the base of a cloud
- large hail or heavy rain with a wind shift
- whirling cloud of dust and other materials on the ground
- loud roaring sound that doesn't stop
- flashes near the ground from snapped power lines
- cloud that drops toward the ground

Recovering from a disaster takes time and can be very stressful, but getting through a tornado with no loss of life is the most important thing.

Disastrous Tornadoes

The year 1896 brought a tornado to downtown St. Louis. On May 27, it moved across the Mississippi River. There, it tore off part of a bridge. It passed through the steamboats and damaged them. Then it moved into East St. Louis.

The tornado damaged most of St. Louis City Center and destroyed many homes. It killed 225 people and was the costliest tornado at the time. The half-hour tornado would likely be rated today as an EF-4.

On March 18, 1925, the deadly Tri-State tornado pushed through Missouri, Illinois, and Indiana. It spent more than three hours on the ground, killing 747 people as it moved across the three states.

The 219 mile (352 kilometer) path it cut was up to three-quarters of a mile (one kilometer) wide. Winds were thought to be more than 300 miles per hour (483 kilometers per hour). Today, it would be rated an EF-5. Hundreds were injured and 15,000 homes were destroyed.

The St. Louis, Missouri, tornado on May 27, 1896, was one of the deadliest and most destructive storms documented in the US.

A tornado hit Tupelo, Mississippi, on April 5, 1936. The next day, two tornadoes joined together over Gainesville, Georgia. The two-day death count reached 454 and hundreds were injured.

The worst tornado disaster in New England took place on June 9, 1953. Worcester, Massachusetts, was hit by a tornado, killing 90 and injuring more than 1,000 people. It tore apart homes and filled streets with debris.

The 1953 tornado in Worcester, Massachusetts, caused 80 deaths, injured about 800 people, and cost millions of dollars. More than 2,500 people were left homeless.

April 27, 2011, brought an EF-4 tornado to Tuscaloosa, Alabama. The spring and summer of 2011 had the most deadly and destructive tornadoes in US history. About 551 people died that day when more than 200 tornadoes spread through the Southeast.

This EF-4 tornado had winds of 190 miles per hour (306 kilometers per hour) and killed 65 people. Many homes were destroyed. The tornado dropped from an EF-2 down to an EF-0. It gathered strength again and became an EF-4.

The 2011 Tuscaloosa, Alabama, tornado was formed by a supercell in Newton County, Alabama, at 2:54 p.m and continued until 10:18 p.m. This supercell traveled about 380 miles (612 kilometers).

The 2011 Joplin, Missouri, tornado was the single deadliest tornado since official records were begun in 1950. It initiated the development of recommendations for improving the design of buildings and shelters.

Top winds of 200 miles per hour (322 kilometers per hour) from a tornado destroyed Joplin, Missouri, on May 22, 2011. It killed 162 people and caused billions of dollars in damage. The EF-5 tornado reached three-quarters of a mile wide (1.2 kilometers) and covered six miles (10 kilometers).

An EF-5 tornado passed through Newcastle, Oklahoma, and then moved on to Moore on May 20, 2013. The mile-wide (1.61 kilometer) tornado was on the ground for 40 minutes. It extended 14 miles (23 kilometers).

Moore residents had about a 30 minute warning before it hit. The tornado damaged several elementary schools. The city hospital lost its top half and injured patients had to be moved to another location. The storm killed 24 people.

Tornadoes today are still deadly, but more people are receiving warning and taking cover earlier. Keeping up with news alerts lets you know what's coming.

Improvements in construction and building materials are another way to stay safer in a tornado. Building codes are stricter and encourage better design of sturdier structures that withstand debris in areas frequently hit by tornadoes.

FEMA community relations workers discuss building safety in a Home Depot store. FEMA offers guidelines for reinforced safe rooms to use for shelter during a tornado.

This safe room, built by Mell Huffman of Moore, Oklahoma, one month before the Moore tornado, saved the lives of four people and three dogs during the EF-5 tornado on May 20, 2013.

Making a plan and heeding the warnings can help save lives. Nobody can stop a tornado, but people can prepare and know where to go when disaster strikes.

On May 31, 2013, Tim Samaras, an engineer; Paul, his son; and Carl Young, a meteorologist, died in the El Reno, Oklahoma, tornado. A strong circulation inside the rain-covered tornado turned northwest toward the car they were using to track the storm. The tornado blew their car off the road. They were the first storm researchers to die in their storm-chasing work.

The three respected storm chasers died when their car was hit by a tornado formed from the larger El Reno tornado in 2013. Tornadoes can be deadly if they change direction suddenly or form new tornadoes.

Predicting the Storm

The National Weather Center, housed on the University of Oklahoma campus in Norman, Oklahoma, brings together people from NOAA, state organizations, and the university to work together to improve knowledge about Earth's changing atmosphere and how the changes relate to the weather.

Studying tornadoes is a difficult but important job. Much of the information known is determined by the National Severe Storms Laboratory (NSSL). This research lab is in the National Weather Center in Norman, Oklahoma. Scientists there find ways to improve tornado forecasts and warnings.

Meteorologists and researchers work together to develop instruments and collect data for tornado forecasting. Engineers play a part in tornado studies and instrument design. Some University of Oklahoma faculty, staff, and students participate in the research. **Interdisciplinary** teams also contribute.

Researchers use weather tools during thunderstorms to study the exact actions that occur to form tornadoes. They study what makes storms break apart. They look at why some storms don't produce tornadoes while others do.

NSSL researchers made a three-dimensional computer model of a tornado. They study how it behaves under different conditions. NSSL works with a national network of radar, too.

Another project is making a computer weather forecast model. The center can send warnings earlier and save lives.

Multiple radars, observations from the Earth's surface and air, lightning detectors, satellites, and forecasting models provide data. Researchers look for patterns that indicate tornadoes.

The scientists also use supercomputers, data, and meteorology to make accurate forecasts. They study why tornadoes form in certain places. Video from storm chases and Doppler radar help them understand tornadoes better. Mobile technology allows them to work in any location.

High-tech supercomputers help meteorologists forecast the weather more accurately.

The Doppler On Wheels Project allows scientists to observe tornado winds and other weather phenomena in three dimensional detail.

Doppler radar is important equipment. It measures wind speed and wind direction in a thunderstorm. It also measures how hard it is raining. Doppler-on-wheels (DOW), or mobile radar attached to trucks or trailers, makes on-site observations near tornadoes. DOW measures details of tornadoes and wind speed in the air.

TOTO

A portable weather-sensing device named after Dorothy's dog in the movie *The Wizard of Oz* was a 300 pound (136 kilogram) aluminum barrel with tools to measure wind speed, pressure, and water in the air. The researchers rolled the Totable Tornado Observatory (TOTO) off the truck, turned it on, and left. In 1984 it managed to get information from a weak tornado, but was retired soon after.

Environmental researchers use portable weather stations like this one for short-term information. They hold wind sensors and provide instruments for measuring temperature, humidity, and air pressure.

Portable weather stations also measure wind speed, wind direction, temperature, moisture in the air, and air pressure. Small, heavy, wind-resistant tools called turtles are built to stand up to tornado wind speeds.

A turtle is full of sensors that collect tornado data for scientists.

Turtles measure temperature, pressure, and water in the air at ground level. They are put about 100-250 yards (91-229 meters) apart in a tornado's path. New work with them holds promise.

Forecasts made by meteorology and computer science are being studied. Warnings could be made on a numerical basis.

Early **simulator** tornado studies began in the 1960s. Neil Ward of NSSL built smoke funnel chambers in his house. Ted Fujita made a simulator and studied air speed and pressure.

Storm chasers add to the current information. Early chasers included Neil Ward, David Hoadley, and Roger Jensen. They used their data to build lab simulations. NWS members study tornado damage, along with experts in damage surveying.

Storm spotters report weather information to the NWS office. Chasers are mobile and travel long distances to study storms.

Storm chasers risk their lives to collect data and images of tornadoes. Becoming a storm chaser requires special training and they must know safety techniques if they are caught in a storm.

Representatives from FEMA, the NWS, and other organizations plan together to help the people of Moore, Oklahoma, after the EF5 tornado that heavily damaged the city on May 20, 2013.

As more data arrives, the science of tornado forecasting improves. The purpose of this research and work is to keep more people safe when tornadoes occur.

Fast Fact

The first documented tornado forecast by meteorologists happened in 1948. Two Air Force officers noticed a weather pattern that developed a tornado. When similar weather conditions happened a few days later, they issued a forecast and safety precautions were set up. A tornado later hit the base.

How You Can Help When Disaster Strikes

- Look up your city or town and learn if it is in a tornado area
- Get your family to make a tornado plan
- Prepare an emergency kit to be ready if a tornado comes
- Volunteer with your family to help at an organization that serves food or passes out water after a disaster
- Donate money to agencies like the American Red Cross, Doctors Without Borders, or the Salvation Army
- Donate clothing, food, or other asked-for items
- Organize a fundraiser
- Organize a community event to raise awareness about tornadoes
- Volunteer at a pet shelter that helps pets lost during storms

American Red Cross

Disaster Relief

The Red Cross provides aid to residents of Caruthersville, Missouri after an outbreak of tornadoes from a supercell on April 2, 2006, brought damage to many cities across the region. A total of 66 tornadoes spread over seven states.

Glossary

Doppler radar (DAH-pluhr RAY-dahr): an instrument using radio waves to determine how heavy precipitation is, its speed, hail size, and rainfall amounts

forecast (FOR-kast): predicting the coming weather using data

Fujita Scale (foo-JEE-tah SKALE): a rating system for tornado severity

funnel cloud (FUHN-uhl KLOUD): a rotating column of air that doesn't touch ground and does no damage

interdisciplinary (in-tuhr-DIS-uh-pluhn-ner-ee): including subjects in many areas

mesocyclone (mes-oh-SYE-klone): a circulation of air inside a supercell

meteorologists (mee-tee-uh-RAH-luh-jists): scientists who study and forecast weatherr

simulator (SIM-yuh-lay-tur): a machine that lets you practice a condition that performs like the real situation

supercells (SOO-pur-selz): rotating thunderstorms with a balanced circulation

updraft (UHP-draft): an upward moving current of air

wall clouds (WAWL KLOUDS): downward bulges of air below a cloud that often gives rise to tornadoes

Index

Show What You Know

1. Describe the weather conditions necessary for a tornado to form.
2. Discuss the reason so many tornadoes take place in the central US along the region called Tornado Alley.
3. Explain why data on tornadoes can't always be exact.
4. Name three places you go and explain where and why you would choose to shelter in each of the three places.
5. Create your own family tornado plan and discuss it.

Websites to Visit

www.sciencekids.co.nz/sciencefacts/weather/tornado.html
www.ready.gov/kids/know-the-facts/tornado
www.fema.gov/media-library-data/a4ec63524f9fd1fa5d72be63bd6b29cf/
FEMA_FS_tornado_508_8-15-13.pdf

About the Author

As a child, Shirley Duke was fearful of tornadoes, but after she learned more about them, she knew what to do if one did come nearby and wasn't worried after that. Tornado warnings were common while she was growing up in Dallas and she even saw a few tornadoes. She likes learning about nature's cycles and how weather works.

Meet The Author!
www.meetREMauthors.com

PHOTO CREDITS: Cover © Warren Faidley/Corbis; Title Page © fergery; page 2, 3 © Tokarsky; page 8, 11, 13, 14, 40, 41, 42, 44 © NOAA; page 9, 11 © Minerva Studio; page 12 © Vanessa Ezekowitz/Wikipedia; page 13 © Positiveflash; page 15, 41 © Jim Reed / Science Source; page 17 © Andrew J Oldaker/Wikipedia; page 18 © anthonyspencer; page 20 © golfadi; page 22 © gabes1976; page 23 © Dustie; page 24 © Lightningtodd, SeanMartin, Clintspencer; page 25 © Jocelyn Augustino/FEMA; page 26, 28, 29 © George Armstrong/FEMA; page 27, 31 © W. Steve Shepard Jr.; page 30, 38 © Andrea Booher/FEMA; page 32 © Mr. Steve Nicklas/NOS/NGS/NOAA; page 33 © NOAA/Strauss; page 34 © Bettmann/Corbis; page 35 © Thilo Parg; page 36 © James Pauls • eyecare LLC; page 37 © Rossyveth Rey-Berríos/FEMA; page 38 © National Weather Service Office in Norman, Oklahoma/Wikipedia; page 39 © Tyler Arbogast; page 41 © traveler1116; page 42 © Laubact/Wikipedia; page 43 © Mike Berger / Science Source; page 44 © NOAA/James Murnan; page 45 © Patsy Lynch/FEMA

Edited by: Keli Sipperley
Cover and interior design by: Jen Thomas

Library of Congress PCN Data

Tornadoes / Shirley Duke
(Devastating Disasters)
ISBN 978-1-63430-426-9 (hard cover)
ISBN 978-1-63430-526-6 (soft cover)
ISBN 978-1-63430-616-4 (e-Book)
Library of Congress Control Number: 2015931739

Printed in the United States of America, North Mankato, Minnesota

Also Available as: